AF825227

A REASON FOR Hope

When You've Been Abused

A REASON FOR
Hope

When You've Been Abused

Andre Bustanoby

Here's Life Publishers

Published by
HERE'S LIFE PUBLISHERS, INC.
P. O. Box 1576
San Bernardino, CA 92402

HLP Product No. 951384
© 1986, Andre Bustanoby
All rights reserved.
Printed in the United States of America.

Library of Congress Cataloging in Publication Data

Bustanoby, André
A reason for hope. When you've been abused.

Includes bibliographical references.
1. Child molesting — United States. 2. Incest victims — United States. 3. Adult child abuse victims — United States. I. Title.
HQ72.U53B86 1986 362.7'044 86-9837
ISBN 0-89840-151-8 (pbk.)

FOR MORE INFORMATION, WRITE:

L.I.F.E. — P.O. Box A399, Sydney South 2000, Australia
Campus Crusade for Christ of Canada — Box 300, Vancouver, B.C. V6C 2X3, Canada
Campus Crusade for Christ — 103 Friar Street, Reading RG1 1EP, Berkshire, England
Lay Institute for Evangelism — P.O. Box 8786, Auckland 3, New Zealand
Great Commission Movement of Nigeria — P.O. Box 500, Jos, Plateau State Nigeria, West Africa
Life Ministry — P.O. Box/Bus 91015, Auckland Park 2006, Republic of South Africa
Campus Crusade for Christ International — Arrowhead Springs, San Bernardino, CA 92414, U.S.A.

CONTENTS

Chapter 1

THE FAMILY SECRET

Marsha asked to see me alone, without her husband. Though I had explained to her that I usually see married couples together when dealing with marital problems, she said that she was the problem, not her husband, Todd.

I went ahead and gave her an appointment.

"I don't know why Todd doesn't divorce me," she told me when she came for her first session. "I'm not much of a wife."

"Would you help me understand why you say that?" I asked. "That's a pretty harsh judgment of yourself."

What Is the Problem?

Marsha was a very attractive woman. But the personality she exuded to others was listless, unappealing. She was well-dressed and well-groomed, but she looked more like a lifeless mannequin than a woman of thirty who should have been full of life. She had no children, lived in an affluent suburb, and her husband enjoyed a prestigious position in the federal government. She probably was the envy of many women about town, but instead Marsha looked as though she had nothing to live for.

What was the problem? She told me this story.

"I guess you'd say that Todd and I are sexually incompatible. But I really can't blame Todd. I just don't have any interest in sex at all. We've been married for five years, and for the past couple of years, Todd hasn't touched me. He tells me that he finds it difficult to have sexual relations with me when I am obviously not only disinterested but also find it a distasteful experience. He's right. I would be perfectly happy with a sexless marriage, but I know that's too much to expect of him."

Medically, there was no reason for Marsha's aversion to sex. In every other respect she seemed to be a normal thirty-year-old woman, with the exception of her extremely poor self-image.

"I don't know why Todd married me in the first place," she said. "He had his pick of any number of women who had a lot more going for them than I. Yet he chose me."

Marsha pondered in silence what she had said. Finally, she spoke. "I guess I had hoped that, by marrying him, I'd feel better about myself. He seemed to see something in me even though I didn't."

This was quite a remarkable statement since Marsha had won a couple of beauty pageants and popularity contests in college and had graduated with honors. Yet, she was saying something I have heard over and over again from accomplished people. How we perceive and feel about ourselves often has nothing to do with our accomplishments.

As our first session together drew to a close, I didn't know Marsha any better than when she walked through the door. Yes, I had learned that she had no interest in sex and that she had a poor self-image in spite of her beauty, accomplishments and marriage to an important man. But she seemed unable or unwilling to tell me more. She simply didn't know what her problem could be.

I suggested that we do some projective testing in our next session. This was the kind of test that would help me understand how she viewed life. We would start with a sentence-completion test.

Marsha was not enthusiastic. "I really don't know if it will help," she said. "I think that Todd should go ahead and divorce me. Why doesn't he just tell the judge that I can't perform as a wife?"

I had the uneasy feeling that Marsha was seeking counseling, not to solve her marital problem, but rather to gain some professional support for her belief that she was beyond help.

This is a problem that medical doctors and counselors encounter frequently. But Marsha agreed to return in a few days and pursue the matter further.

A Painful Trip Home.

When I saw Marsha again, I immediately started the sentence-completion test. Rather than have her write her responses, I gave the sentences to her orally because I wanted to discuss any of her responses that sounded significant.

I questioned her over a period of several weeks, and during that time, I noticed a pattern emerging. It centered on responses about mother, father and home life.

For example, one sentence stated, "I used to feel I was being held back by . . ."

Marsha responded, "My parents."

Another question probed further: "As a child my greatest fear was . . ."

Marsha replied, "Abandonment."

But the sentence and response that most aroused my curiosity was this one: "My father always . . ." Marsha's response was, "Depended on me."

I asked her to tell me more. In what way did he depend on her? Marsha opened up and told me something about her family life.

"My father was a career Army enlisted man. When I was little, he was away a lot. I think he was overseas. And then when he was at home, he had to travel a lot.

"Mom made a life of her own. She's not living now. She died several years ago in an auto accident. But she was a buyer for a department store — a very bright and ambitious woman. She soon rose through the ranks and became an executive in a chain of stores. I guess you could say that she was a 'better man' than my dad.

"He was content to take promotions as they came. Mom didn't have much respect for him, probably because of this. She seemed to be saying by her behavior that she'd make something of her life, even if he didn't.

"Mom was away much of the time, too. I spent a lot of time with baby-sitters or at nursery school. I was a good student, because Mom expected it of me. She told me that women are to make it in life on their own merit and not because of the men they are married to.

"When I was older, about twelve or thirteen, I saw more of Dad. I really felt sorry for him. Though he was a sergeant, he wasn't your typical drillmaster type. He was trained as a cook and worked in food services.

"We had a pretty good relationship for a while. He'd usually be home from work when I came home from school, and he'd spend time with me. In fact, he taught me everything I know about cooking.

"I never saw my mother. She was too busy out in the world making her mark.

"Dad seemed to get a lot of pleasure out of the way I kept house. I really am a good homemaker. And he took particular relish in the meals that I'd cook for him. I guess I was a source of pride to him and gave him the feeling that he did something right. He had taught me to be a good cook and homemaker.

"As I grew older, our relationship cooled. By the time I was sixteen, Dad and I were pretty far apart."

That was the end of the story as far as Marsha was concerned. There was no explanation as to why she and her dad became estranged. She acted as though there was no more to tell.

I quizzed her about this, but she had a hard time remembering. Then with some annoyance she said, "I guess it was his drinking that did it." Again, she volunteered no further information.

After some silence, I asked if she would tell me more about it. Her annoyance at me was more evident than ever.

"I'd get home from school, and he would be drinking. He wasn't falling down drunk, but he was intoxicated."

Again, silence.

"Would you tell me more?" I asked.

"What does this have to do with anything?" Marsha asked. "The man was a poor, pathetic drunk. And he didn't even have a wife to comfort him. She was out making her mark on the world!"

Then Marsha turned her anger on me. "Let's get on with this stupid test. Next question, please!"

We sat in silence for a short while as Marsha waited impatiently to answer the last of the questions and end the session.

"I'd like to talk more about your dad and his drinking," I said, looking down at my pad.

"There's nothing more to say," Marsha replied in an even, firm tone of voice.

We sat in silence. Finally I said, "This reminds me of a line from one of Shakespeare's plays," gently chiding her.

"What do you mean?"

" 'Thou protesteth too much.' You tell me that there's no more to the story than what you have said, but your anger suggests that I've touched on a sensitive subject."

"All right, so I am angry!" she replied. "Do you have any idea what it's like to be fourteen years old and hold a father in your arms who feels unloved and unlovable, crying because he feels like a failure? Where was my mother all this time?"

Marsha was really steaming by now. Her anger at her mother was perfectly understandable. This was a burden to a fourteen-year-old girl. But her response failed to answer some important questions: What was it about her dad's drinking that she didn't like? How did her relationship with her father affect her at this critical stage of her psychosexual development? Did it have anything to do with her disinterest in sex?

The Family Secret.

We sat in silence for some time. I knew that I had to ask the unaskable and speak the unspeakable.

"I imagine that your dad really missed having a wife who could be understanding and comforting. In fact, when he was drinking, I imagine that the family boundaries got kind of fuzzy to him."

Again, we sat in silence. Marsha just looked at me as if to say, "Where are you going with this soliloquy?" But she didn't say a word.

I realized that I would have to carry the conversation. Marsha was not about to help.

"Marsha, what I'm trying to say is that I have a hunch that your dad turned to you to fill the vacuum left by a wife who was not there. In situations like this where there is drinking and the sexual boundaries are fuzzy, a father sometimes turns to his daughter to fill his sexual needs."

Marsha's body became tense and rigid. She grasped the arms of the chair as though she were hanging on for her life. She crossed her legs tightly and looked at the floor.

We sat in silence, and as the clock ticked away, we both could feel the tension building. But there was little that I could say. It was a time of decision for Marsha. Did she have a family secret? If so, would she share it with me?

A Soul In Agony.

I, too, looked at the floor. I didn't want Marsha to feel intimidated by a stare or anything that might be construed as pressure. I just wanted her to know that I was ready to talk if she was.

When she reached into her purse, I looked up to see what she was doing. She was pulling out a tissue; tears were trickling down her cheeks.

My impulse was to reach over, take her hand and reassure her. At first, I checked the impulse, fearing that touching might be inappropriate.

But my empathy won out; I couldn't leave her comfortless. I reached over, grasped her hand and said, "Marsha, it's okay to cry."

The dam burst. With great, heaving sobs, Marsha cried, "I'm so ashamed. I'm so ashamed."

She didn't have to say anything further. We just held hands and wept together. The family secret was no longer a secret.

Chapter 2
NO LONGER ALONE

The sexual abuse of children and adolescents has been one of the best kept secrets in the history of the American family — at least until ten or fifteen years ago. Marsha's courage in bringing her secret out into the open — and the courage of hundreds of thousands of people like her — has awakened Americans to this awful plight and moved many to action in behalf of its victims.

Not only is an aware nation beginning to do something about the problem, but those who have been abused are discovering that they are not alone. Adults who were abused as children are finding out that they are not a rare social aberration, nor are they perverts who ought to hide their shame and guilt. They are *victims* who have suffered in silence and, because of their silence, they have had to bear their torment alone. They have found no comfort or help, simply because they are convinced that something is wrong with *them,* and they don't want anyone to know.

The Magnitude of the Problem.

Incidents of sexual abuse can only be estimated, because many of the abused choose to suffer in silence rather than reveal their terrible secret. One study estimates that one in four girls will be a victim of sexual abuse by the time she is eighteen. Boys face a similar risk.[1] Another study estimates that at least thirty-three percent of all females have been victimized by an incestuous father.[2]

Researchers have discovered that the usual stereotype of the child abuser — a dirty old man who prowls playgrounds and school yards in search of victims — is not accurate. Most often the abuser is someone acquainted with the child. Children do, indeed, need to be warned about strangers, because they can present a real danger. But it is the family member who poses the greatest threat.

Cases In Point.

Sexual abuse of children is found in families of every economic stratum, from the very poor to the very rich. And it involves children of all ages.

Several years ago, Cincinnati Children's Hospital treated 78 children for symptoms, signs or complaints of sexual abuse during a one-year period. The children's ages ranged from nearly two years to twelve. Children from one to five years of age made up almost half of those treated.

Fifteen children were treated for gonorrhea. One five-year-old female had secondary syphilis in addition to gonorrhea. One nine-year-old female was treated for gonorrhea twice.

Case #1. One case involved Tina, a 7-year-old white female brought to the emergency room by her mother, Mrs. C. Medical examination found that Tina had vaginal irritation and a ruptured hymen.

Suspicion of sexual abuse was confirmed when Tina told her mother that her stepfather had been having intercourse with her and that she had witnessed his masturbation with ejaculation. The stepfather, unemployed for approximately five months, had been taking care of Tina after school while her mother worked.

Mrs. C's first husband had been physically abusive to her, so when she remarried, she was determined not to make the same mistake again. She married Mr. C, a weak man who was seldom employed.

When Mr. C's sexual abuse of Tina surfaced, he was banished from the house. Tina, who felt affection for him, took the blame for his banishment. To make matters worse, Mrs. C not only refused to discuss the abuse with Tina, but she also compounded Tina's-guilt feelings by frequently declaring her love for her husband in Tina's presence.

Preliminary court proceedings were difficult for Tina. She cried and refused to testify against her stepfather. She told her mother that she loved him and wanted him home.

Mrs. C divorced her husband. She later entered a therapy group where she gained insight and support. It is not known, however, if Tina received any help.[3]

Case #2. Mary was a fifteen-year-old white female whose mother died when she was twelve. She came to the attention of juvenile authorities when her younger brother, age fourteen, repeatedly ran away from home. The boy finally disclosed to the authorities that he could not stand living at home because of what his father was doing to his sister.

Investigation disclosed that when Mary's mother died, her father told her that she was now "the woman of the house," and that he expected her to take over where her mother left off. Over a period of time he instructed her in her womanly duties, which included sleeping with him.

Though sexual relations did not begin immediately, Mary was subject to what therapists call "positive coercion." This is not to be confused with seduction, which involves the willingness of the person seduced. Positive coercion pressures the victim to cooperate but does not use threat or physical force. It is effective when the victimizer is a parent, stepparent or another authority figure who uses his position of authority to intimidate the victim into cooperating.

Mary's father was eventually sent to prison. She and her brother were placed in foster homes. They both received counseling.

Positive Coercion and Sexual Problems.

Recent studies show that as many as one in four women have been sexually molested. Females who were molested as children tend to have sexual problems as adults when there was positive, rather than negative, coercion. Negative coercion involves the use of threat or physical force. According to a study of 952 college students, 23 percent of the girls who had been molested stated that they had sexual difficulties as adults. Their sexual difficulties were rooted in the guilt they felt from succumbing to molestation that took place without the threat of physical force. Conversely, when the victim was coerced with verbal threats or physical attack, she absolved herself of culpability.[4]

Other findings in the study revealed:

- Heterosexual molestation was nine times greater than homosexual molestation.

- The molester of female children was likely to be a relative of great interpersonal power, such as a parent, grandparent, aunt or uncle. This was not true in the case of male-child molesters.

- Females were decidedly negative about their childhood sexual experiences.

In the case of molested males, researchers found that the majority had been molested by females. This challenges the common idea that male children are most often molested by pathological homosexuals.

Other findings in the study revealed:

- Males were much less likely than females to talk about being molested by family members.

- Males were generally not as negative about their experience as females were.

- Casual contact [as in playful physical touching and in sitting and lying together] was the usual way males were introduced to sexual experience.

- Researchers think that the incidence of male molestation is much higher than once believed. It may be as high as one male for every two females.[5]

In spite of the startling statistics, the study did offer hope. The vast majority of the girls (77 percent of those molested) either were able to overcome the negative consequences of their experience or did not ever develop physical or psychological problems. Furthermore, as a result of the attention that this problem has been given, the medical and psychological professions have been able to develop methods of therapeutic intervention that can help those who carry the trauma of sexual abuse into adulthood.

Help and Hope.

The professional community has learned a great deal about helping those who have been abused. As a result of this help, victims are finding new hope. Those who seek professional help can expect the following:

1. *To be heard.* Those who have been sexually abused often don't know what it means to be listened to in a nonjudgmental way. This is particularly true when the child has been raised in a home or church-going environment where everyone is quick to judge and spirituality is measured by outward appearance, rather than by inward reality. The child from this background is reluctant to reveal his or her secret because of fear of what others will think.

The therapist, especially the Christian therapist who bases his treatment on a foundation of biblical love, authority and truth, makes himself available as an honest and trusted technician. Acquainted with the trauma of sexual abuse, he is able to join the victim in his or her loneliness and isolation. He is neither repelled with disgust nor impelled to judge. He is able to listen with an understanding ear and convey hope for recovery based on his experience in treating the problem.

2. *To have success.* Feelings of helplessness and failure are primary ingredients of despair. The therapist is able to help his client achieve reachable goals. The trauma of sexual abuse, which is overwhelming to the victim, can be explained in such a way that the client understands what happened, why, and what can be done about it. Often, the client experiences a profound release from guilt just by being able to understand what

happened. In cases of sexual dysfunction such as that experienced by Marsha in chapter 1, some of the best sex therapy comes from this kind of release.

3. *To experience better communication.* One of the key problems the victim of sexual abuse has is difficulty in communication. This person has been trained by the abuser *not* to talk, particularly about things that may be embarrassing or may present a threat to harmony in the family system. In therapy, the victim of sexual abuse discovers that he or she may talk about anything and everything without self-consciousness or fear of what disclosure may bring.

4. *To see a ray of hope.* The victim of sexual abuse is often so overwhelmed by trauma that he or she cannot even begin to hope. Having worked through the experience of sexual abuse with others, the therapist is able to give assurance that the trauma is something that one can and will overcome. Without violating confidentiality, he is able to share what others have done to overcome the trauma.

The Christian therapist with a good grasp of theology is able to do more. He is able to integrate the victim's experience with God's plan for that person's life.

In 1981, a young woman by the pen name of Deborah Roberts wrote a book titled *Raped.* It is the story of how she was brutally raped while serving God in an inner-city ministry in Chicago. Not only did she experience the horror of rape, but she also faced the brutal insensitivity of the court system. Her nightmare lasted ten years. Again and again, Deborah asked the question that all women who are sexually abused ask: "Why, God? Why me?"

I can't second-guess God, but I do know this: God has used her powerfully to help hundreds of other women who have suffered as she. I have been able to use her book to bring hope to others.

Could it be that God wants to take such a tragedy and turn it to triumph? Could it be that he wants to show the world that in spite of the evil of sexual abuse, He's still in charge?

I'm reminded of the story in the Bible of the man born blind (John 9:1-12). Jesus' disciples wanted to know if his blindness was due to his sin or that of his parents'. Jesus answered that neither had sinned. He said it happened so the work of God might be displayed in his life (John 9:3).

Though Deborah, Marsha and thousands of others have been the victims of sexual abuse, God often permits tragedy — even this kind — to show His power. Perhaps you or someone you know has suffered in a similar way and is now praying that God would use the traumatic experience to His glory. Could it be, perhaps, that God's call to triumph over sexual abuse by His power and grace is the answer to this prayer? This was Marsha's experience.

---

1. Linda Sanford, "Protecting Children Against Child Molesters," *Current Research on Children,* 2 Vol. (New York: ATCOM, Inc., Publishers, 1983), 2:53.
2. Dr. Alvin A. Rosenfeld, "Psychologists Ask Female Patients About Incest," *Current Research,* 2:60
3. Jerilyn A. Shamroy, "A Perspective on Childhood Sexual Abuse," *Social Work,* (March 1980), p. 128.
4. Kim Stoll, "Positive Coercion Causes Adult Sexual Problems in Molested Girls," *Current Research,* 2:55.
5. Ibid., 2:55-56.

Chapter 3

THE ANATOMY OF INCEST

After Marsha's traumatic second session in counseling, she returned to talk further about her experience with her father. The "family secret" had been brought out into the open, and now understanding and healing could begin. But if I was to be of any help to Marsha I would have to help her understand what had happened to her. The guilt and shame that she admitted to feeling made her think that something was terribly wrong with her. Sexually abused women like Marsha often feel that they are perverted people.

Marsha had to understand the anatomy of incest if she was to be free of guilt. My job was to help her see and understand six key factors that worked together to cause her traumatic experience.[1] We began by discussing her father's problem with alcohol. "Dad always had a drinking problem. Though I didn't like him to drink, his drinking never caused any serious problems for me — until I was fourteen," said Marsha.

"I came home from school one day, and he was lying on the couch drunk. He told me to come over and sit by him, which I did. He took my hand in his and began to cry and tell me what a failure he had been as a father. I put my arms around him, hugged him and told him that I didn't think he had failed me as a father.

"We held each other briefly, and then he put his hand on my breast. Instinctively, I drew back. He took his hand away, buried his face in his hands and sobbed. He didn't have to say a word. I knew that he was feeling even worse about himself than before, and I felt so sorry for him.

"Suddenly, my sorrow turned to rage — against my mother. Where was she when her husband needed her? Why did she treat him so mean? Maybe my dad was right when he claimed that she drove him to drink. Though I didn't like his sexual advance, I was sorry that I had rebuffed him.

"Dad drank some more and passed out on the couch. I spent the rest of the day in my room, listening to music and thinking. When Mom came home, she came to my room and said, 'Hi.' The only other thing she had to say was, 'I see your drunken father has passed out on the couch.' She ignored him and went to her room, where she spent the rest of the evening.

"The next day when I came home from school, Dad was there, as usual. Neither of us said a word about what had happened the day before. He was warm and kind, but he kept his distance from me. As far as I know, he had not been drinking. It was almost as though the incident that occurred the day before had happened to someone else."

As Marsha told her story, a pattern quickly became evident. When her father was sober, he was a model father. But when he was drunk, he would approach Marsha sexually. The first few times she rebuffed him, and his response was always the same: profound grief over what he had done, abject groveling for her forgiveness and more drinking until he passed out. Marsha said that she felt tremendous guilt — not over her father's sexual advances — but for adding to her father's self-hatred and feelings of failure. She couldn't stand to see him grovel.

At this point in her life, Marsha could no longer disguise her anger at her mother. Though Marsha said nothing to her about what was going on with her father, she bitterly criticized her mother for her absence from the home and for how she treated Marsha's dad.

When verbally attacked by her daughter, Marsha's mother would defend herself on both issues. She rationalized her neglect by arguing that she had to work if the family was going to make ends meet. *She* was going to make something of her life, even if her husband didn't.

But Marsha was never able to broach the subject of her father's sexual behavior or needs with her mother. "How does a fourteen-year-old girl tell her mother that she is failing her husband sexually?" she asked me.

The time came when Marsha gave in to her father. "It's hard to explain," she said. "I didn't want him touching me sexually, but I just couldn't stand what happened when I rebuffed him — to see my father sobbing, drooling and groveling. At those times, my fury at my mother was incredible! One day something snapped. I couldn't see my father torture himself any longer. I knew that the next time he approached me sexually, I'd give in. And I did.

"We didn't have intercourse, but he kissed me and fondled me. I didn't like what was happening, but I didn't feel that I was being sexually abused. I was preoccupied with anger at my mother for not being there when her husband needed her. And when it was over, at least my father didn't cry. He drank some more and passed out.

"I remember rationalizing that this was a lot better than going through his groveling. And I tried to think that what we were doing was not sex but my meeting a need he had — a need my mother refused to meet. I began to develop the ability to emotionally detach myself from what we were doing, and in time, it became intercourse."

Alcohol was an essential ingredient in this incestuous relationship. It provided an excuse for her father's behavior. Marsha also was able to rationalize that it was the alcohol, not her father, who was to blame for what he did.

This rationalization was reinforced by the fact that when her father was not drinking, he was a model father. And when he was sober, not a word was said about his sexual behavior toward her. He was able to create a schizophrenic situation where it was not he, but someone else, who was abusing his daughter.

However, the problem of incest in Marsha's family was not just a simple matter of her father's inhibitions being torn down by alcohol as Marsha supposed. The connection between drinking and deviance is more subtle.

As I began to explain to Marsha, there were *six* key factors working together in her family that caused the incestuous relationship.

1. *Her father's incestuous personality.* Contrary to popular belief, the typical incestuous male is not a sociopath or psychopath. He is not a person who obviously is "sick in the head." He usually gives the appearance of normalcy.

But aside from that, there are some personality types that typify the incestuous male. One personality type is the tyrannical male who dominates the family and keeps his wife dependent on him and afraid. His tyrannical behavior and intimidation of the family make coercion of the daughter possible.

Because of the stereotype of this particular personality, feminist literature is quick to blame a male-dominated society for the evil of incest. But the problem of incest is not that easily explained. All incestuous males are not tyrants. Marsha's father is representative of another group that is inhibited, shy and ineffectual. He has difficulty maintaining social relationships. This type of man often is dependent on his wife for emotional and, all too frequently, financial support.

Marsha's father did not feel good about himself. He agreed that his wife was a better man than he, at least according to the stereotype of the aggressive male in American culture. She showed far more get-up-and-go. She was ambitious and assertive, and she knew what she wanted out of life.

It was obvious to Marsha that her dad was suffering from a poor self-image and that he needed a lot of positive strokes. It also was obvious that her mother was not about to give her father these needed strokes. In fact, her mother was openly contemptuous of the man.

This set up a lethal chemistry within the family relationships. While Marsha's mother was proving she was a better man than her husband, Marsha had an opportunity to counter this by showing her mother that she was a better woman than her mother. Marsha had the opportunity to give her dad the love and affirmation that her mother would not. There was nothing immoral about her behavior. It was the proper response of a loving human being to someone who was suffering.

What's more, this was happening at a time in Marsha's psychosexual development when she would become naturally more competitive with her mother and begin to think of herself as a woman who had the ability to run a house and take care of a man. Though she was not thinking in sexual terms, gradually circumstances were pushing her into the position of a second-string wife, prompting her to provide for all her father's needs.

This situation is found in many homes that are not incestuous. A daughter often becomes a second-string wife who takes care of her father. But Marsha's father was a weak man who did not have much moral fiber, a condition made worse by the fact that he was an alcoholic.

2. *Inadequate maternal protection*. Marsha's mother also played a significant role in the scenario. The absence of the mother in incestuous families has long been recognized as one of the factors that contribute to sexual abuse. Sometimes that absence is due to the wife's sickness or extended hospitalization. Marsha's mother *chose* to be absent so that she could get on with her own life.

Women who find themselves in this mother's position can readily identify with her need to save herself from an unmotivated, alcoholic husband who would discourage and demotivate her, too. But a fourteen-year-old girl can't understand what it means to live with a man like that. Indeed, she sees him as a poor, pathetic soul who needs the care and affection of a wife. It is not unusual for a daughter to join forces with her father in taking revenge against the mother's abandonment.

Researchers have discovered that, in some cases, incest becomes a mutually agreeable solution to both husband and wife. For such a couple, it relieves the wife's guilt caused by denying sex to her husband, and it also meets the husband's deprived sexual needs.

In fairness to wives, we should not conclude that they cynically condone incest because it serves their needs. Incest in families develops far more subtly. But it is important to point out that incest is a *family* problem. When women like Marsha whip themselves with shame and guilt, they clearly do not recognize the family dynamic that includes the behavior of the mother. Marsha's anger at her mother was well-founded and was one of the major issues we needed to deal with if Marsha were to be healed. However, it would be complicated by the fact that her mother was dead.

3. *Fear of abandonment.* Another factor that promoted incest in Marsha's family was fear of abandonment. Marsha felt as though her mother had abandoned her. And though she did not consciously attempt to keep her father from abandoning her by submitting to his sexual overtures, she struggled with this at the subconscious level. Both sets of her grandparents were divorced. The extended family of aunts, uncles and cousins was not close. It was a fragmented family, structurally and emotionally.

Early in Marsha's life her dad had been absent a lot. She didn't get to know him until she was older when he was home more.

The fear of abandonment is one factor that permits abuse to go on for years, as it did in Marsha's case. She told me, "I think I was afraid of losing him again. If we were going to have any family at all, it would be Dad and me. Mother just was not part of the family."

Marsha's dad abused her until she went away to a college preparatory academy when she was sixteen. Her mother told her that she wanted to be sure that Marsha was adequately prepared to make her way in life. I think, however, that there was more to it than that. I have a hunch that Marsha's mother suspected Marsha was being sexually abused and, rather than confront the issue, she just sent Marsha off to boarding school.

4. *An isolated incestuous subculture.* Incest generally is thought to exist primarily among the poor and in rural areas. But greater awareness of the problem has revealed that incest is found in every economic stratum of society and in cities as well as in rural areas. Isolation and self-containment are factors that create a climate for incest wherever they are found.

Those who live in cities and high density suburbs know that it is possible to be isolated even though surrounded by other people. When neighbors do not know each other and children don't have friends who are in and out of the house, isolation and self-containment are possible.

Marsha had a few friends at school, but she never had any girl friends over to her house. In the first place, her mother forbade it because of lack of supervision. She said that she could not be there, and she wouldn't trust Marsha's father to supervise them.

But it didn't matter to Marsha anyway. Though she felt sorry for her father, she didn't want her friends to see him drinking. This isolated home life contributed to an incestuous environment.

5. *Opportunity.* Another factor contributing to the emergence of incest in Marsha's family was opportunity. Incestuous fathers often are unemployed. Though Marsha's father was employed, his job was of a nature that placed him at home with his daughter a great deal. The absence of Marsha's mother aggravated the problem further.

6. *Family attitude toward sex.* A final factor is the family attitude toward sex. Marsha's attitude toward sex came primarily from her mother but also was reinforced by her father's behavior. Her mother's attitude toward sex was one of indifference. She expressed no interest in it. All her energies went into her career. According to Marsha, whenever she did say anything about sex, her comments were negative and implied that sex was something men were preoccupied with. The message that Marsha got was that sex was something she would have to put up with when she married.

This had a powerful effect on the way Marsha related to her father and later to her husband. From the beginning she was able to detach herself emotionally from her sexual experience. This enabled her to suffer abuse in silence. But later when she married she found herself sexually unresponsive to her husband as well.

When I pointed this out to Marsha, it answered a question she had about her relationship with her husband. She realized that even though he is an important and talented man, and very different from her father, she often thought of him as a weak person. She realized that she had been trained to think that people who have sexual needs are weak.

She also realized that this unconscious comparison of her husband to her father was another reason she turned off to her husband sexually. In her mind, she was cast once again in the role of a sex object for a weak man, just as she had been as a young girl with her father.

Resisting the Truth.

Marsha's reaction to the anatomy of incest was interesting. She listened to what I had to say, understood it, and even agreed that it described her situation. But to her, it changed nothing.

"My life is a hopeless mess. I have a husband who loves me, but I can't meet his needs. The best thing he can do for himself and me is to divorce me," she said.

What was happening here? Why wasn't she responsive to what I had told her? I discovered that Marsha was suffering from "the ruined woman syndrome."

---

1. David Finkelhor, "Psychological, Cultural and Family Factors in Incest and Family Sexual Abuse," *Journal of Marriage and Family Counseling* (October 1978), pp. 41-49.

Chapter 4

THE RUINED WOMAN SYNDROME

Psychologically speaking, there is no such thing as "the ruined woman syndrome." But it helps me describe what I see in women who have been sexually abused.

Women who have been sexually abused cannot reverse the situation. They cannot become former victims. They were victimized and always will be victims. In spite of this, the majority of women who have been sexually abused (77 percent of the women in the study cited in chapter 2) either showed no adverse effect or were able eventually to overcome the trauma.

But some women are not only profoundly affected by the trauma, but they also seem too quick to accept it. Instead of going through the long, painful process of overcoming it, they learn to cope by accepting the role of the "ruined woman" and playing out what they believe to be the logical consequences of the trauma.

Prostitution As a Way of Coping.

Prostitution is one example of coping with sexual abuse by accepting the role of the ruined woman. In a study of prostitution in San Francisco, a theme that occurred again and again in interviews with prostitutes was, "Once I was ruined by my father for anything decent, what difference did it make if I became a prostitute? Everyone could tell I was ruined."[1]

Prostitutes who voiced this theme were not only convinced that they had been ruined — a condition that could not be reversed — but they also had learned to cope with it by living out what they regarded the role of a ruined woman.

A study in New York City also connected prostitution with a childhood history of sexual abuse. The study reported that the high incidence of prostitution appears to represent a "restitutive-resentful posture" by the victim toward the symbolic father. In other words, these prostitutes are "after" their fathers.[2]

The woman who feels ruined but does not become a prostitute still may be unable to escape her identity as the victim. She often believes that the only way she can cope with her ruined status is to live the role of a ruined woman. She makes peace with herself and society by accepting her role.

Marsha's Resistance.

This is what Marsha had done. She thought that my description of the anatomy of incest was enlightening, but she was not willing to give up her identity as a ruined woman. She insisted that she could not perform sexually and that her husband would have to accept it, too — and divorce her. Though this form of adjustment was unhealthy, it offered a way to cope.

But when I asserted that there was another solution, that she did not have to assume the role of the ruined woman, I stirred up an issue she felt she had laid to rest. Marsha became angry and resistant.

"I told you that I have the solution to the problem. I'm willing to give Todd a divorce. It's obvious that I can't function as a wife, and nothing can be done about it."

Once again, I would have to say some things to Marsha that I didn't want to say. "Marsha, when you first came to see me, I got the distinct impression that you were not coming for help but just to gain professional support for a decision that you already had made — your decision to divorce Todd. I'm sorry, but I can't agree that you're beyond help."

"What have you done to help me?" Marsha shot

back angrily.

"Not a great deal," I confessed. "And I doubt that I will have any success — unless you let me help you."

"Let you help me? No woman in her right mind would turn down help that would save her marriage."

"Why of course she would," I replied. "It happens all the time when people feel that the cure is worse than the affliction."

"What do you mean?"

"Many people who suffer physical pain, from hiatal hernia, for example, choose to live with the condition rather than have surgery. They're afraid that the cure is worse than the condition.

"A hiatal hernia most frequently involves the protrusion of the upper part of the stomach through the opening (hiatus) in the diaphragm where the esophagus passes through the diaphragm to the stomach. The condition can produce pain and discomfort due to the delayed passage of food through the diaphragm into the stomach.

"Surgery does not always relieve the patient's symptoms. But it's true that without surgery they may not be able to eat or sleep normally and may suffer all of their lives. This is the trade-off they make. They suffer the lesser pain rather than what they regard as greater pain, even though it may bring a cure.

"The same thing happens with psychological problems. People learn to live with the problem — and often avoid solving it — because they think the cure is worse than the problem."

"I don't know what you're talking about," Marsha protested. "How could a 'cure,' as you call it, be any worse than what I'm suffering right now?"

"Marsha, part of the cure will be talking about what happened to you," I said.

"What good will talking do?"

"Do you really want to know the answer?" I asked. "I think that you're saying, 'Talking about the problem will do no good — I have made up my mind on that.'"

"No, I haven't made up my mind. What do you propose?"

"What I'd like you to do is sit in on a group that I'm running. It's for women who have been physically and sexually abused. You don't have to say a word if you don't want to. But I'd like you to do this just once before you decide that there's no help for you."

Marsha Meets the Group.

Marsha told me later that the only reason she agreed to attend the group was to shut me up. Since she didn't have to say anything, she felt that she would be safe.

The seven women in the group had been abused in various ways. Four of them had been physically abused — beaten up by their fathers when they were small and later by their husbands. One had been raped, and two had been victims of incest.

I started the group with a statement of purpose. I explained that we were there to examine our feelings and to share those feelings with each other.

We then did some awareness exercises. I asked the women to close their eyes and get in touch with their senses: What were they hearing? How did they feel physically? Was the room temperature comfortable? Did they feel discomfort in any part of their body? How did they feel emotionally? Did they feel relaxed, tense, or anxious? I asked them to open their eyes and look at each member of the group and identify how they felt about that person. Did any of the members make them feel especially comfortable? Did they feel ill at ease with anyone?

The purpose of the exercise was to help them understand how feelings affected our ability to relate to other people comfortably. Lacking awareness of how we feel about other people — and why — is one of the greatest impediments to our ability to build good relationships. It prevents our talking constructively with those who are close to us.

One of the major problems in incestuous families is that they are unable to talk honestly and openly with each other about their feelings. Incest requires a conspiracy of silence among all the members of the family. That silence dulls the awareness of what is going on in the family that pleases or displeases each person. The awareness exercises described above begin to familiarize women with an entirely different approach to people — an approach that is open, honest, aware, and not silent.

After I had given the women sufficient time to look around at the other members of the group I asked them what they had become aware of during the exercises. Three or four of the more verbal women confessed the same feelings: fear and anxiety. They were afraid of what others in the group would think of them if they opened up.

Whenever there is a reluctance to open up, I just wait. The silence seemed interminable. All of the women stared at the floor, including Marsha. Even though I was counseling each of them separately, this was the first time that they had met as a group. I could understand their reluctance to speak up, even though they all knew that the group was for physically and sexually abused women.

Finally, one of the women in the group, Barbara, looked up. Our eyes met; we smiled at each other. I thought that I'd see if she was willing to talk.

"Barbara, are you afraid of what *I'll* think?" I asked. Tears welled up in her eyes, and she shook her head.

I couldn't hold back my tears, because I knew what Barbara had been through. She was the victim of both physical and sexual abuse by a tyrannical father. Her mother also had been beaten.

As we cried together, she reached over and grasped my hand as if to say, "Thank you for understanding." We both cried silently, fully aware of the pain she had been through. Several of the other women were crying by now.

But Marsha didn't cry. She just continued to stare at the floor.

Again, after some silence and the tears had dried, I decided that Barbara would be the one most likely to break the ice.

"Barbara, would you be willing to let the group know why you're afraid to tell them about yourself?"

"I know we're all here for the same reason," she began. "We've all had problems with men. But I don't think anyone else here is responsible, like I am, for her parents' divorce and for sending her father to jail."

Again, silence. As I watched the women, I could tell that one of the other women, Marty, was troubled by what Barbara had said.

"Do you have a problem with that?" I asked Marty.

"Well, yes," she replied. "I don't like Barbara taking full responsibility for what happened. I've been doing this all my married life. I wasn't sexually abused, but when I was small, my father beat up on me. And then I married a man who did the same.

"I've had plastic surgery on my face twice. All the time I'd tell myself that if I had done something different, or if my husband hadn't been drinking, it never would have happened. I once thought that perhaps if he killed me he might change. And you know what? I was *willing* to let him kill me. I loved him that much. It was after he put me in the hospital in intensive care that I realized even my death wouldn't change the man."

Marty's comments really got group interaction flowing. It came as a great surprise to the women in the group that *all of them* secretly felt that they, not the abusive males, were to blame for the physical and sexual abuse they had experienced and for the resulting destruction of their families.

Even Anne, who had been raped, confessed that she felt she was responsible for what had happened, that she was at the wrong place at the wrong time and had not taken adequate measures to repulse the attack.

This touched Marsha. Incredulously she asked, "How can you blame yourself for this? The man was bigger than you; he terrified you. You thought that he was going to kill you, and yet you hold yourself to blame? I don't understand."

Anne just shook her head. Finally, she spoke. "You'd have to go through this experience to understand how I feel."

Marty was visibly annoyed at Marsha. But she didn't say anything. She just glared at Marsha.

"Marty, you might as well put it into words," I said. "You're obviously angry with Marsha."

"Yes, I am. *I* don't understand how *she* can't understand!"

I asked Marty to talk directly to Marsha.

She looked at Marsha and said, "I don't know why you're here, but *I'm* here because I'm tired of accepting the guilt for being beat up on as a child and as a wife. I'm tired of thinking that if only I had done what they wanted or had been more lovable — or something — that they wouldn't have beaten me!"

By now, Marty was shaking with fury. Tears were streaming down her face. "I'm not going to be the victim any longer!" she shouted.

Her body convulsed with sobs. We wept with her — all of us, except Marsha. She seemed shaken by her encounter with Marty. I didn't know what was going on inside of her, but my intuition told me to leave her alone.

After the meeting was over, I saw Marsha single out Anne and apologize to her. Anne smiled and hugged her. "No apology is necessary," she said. Then they talked quietly for some time.

A Ruined Woman No More.

Later on that week, I saw Marsha in a private session. I needed to know what she thought of the group and if she were willing to go again.

"I never thought it would be anything like that," she said. "This business of sharing feelings is scary. Anne and Marty really got to me.

"But tell me what Marty meant when she said that she was not going to be a victim any longer."

I was eager to explain this concept to Marsha. "When a person has been physically or sexually abused, they tend to blame themselves for what happened. It's not a logical or rational response. It's something they *feel.* So, rather than try to do the impossible — to get other people to understand that they feel as though they're to blame — they take a stand that people have a harder time arguing with: They have been ruined. Then, if they are not functioning well, it's perfectly understandable, *because they have been damaged beyond repair.*

"When Marty said that she wasn't going to take the blame any more, she was breaking out of her ruined woman role. By refusing to accept the blame any longer, she was freeing herself of the need to look and act like a ruined woman."

"What do you mean, 'look and act like a ruined woman'?" Marsha asked.

"To do what you're doing," I replied as gently as I could. "You tell me that you cannot function sexually in marriage and that you have a perfectly good reason for it. What you're saying is that you're a ruined woman. What is more, you have a solution: Todd should divorce you. I know that you would find a divorce painful, but in your mind, it's less painful than refusing to take the blame any longer and facing your father and mother with their responsibility in the matter. This is what Marty did — she refused to accept the blame and play the role any longer."

Marsha didn't argue the point. She seemed to understand and accept what I was saying. And she was willing to become part of the group. I knew that it would be just a matter of time when she, with the encouragement of the other women in the group, would stop playing the role of the ruined woman, too, and would face what she didn't want to face — her parents' responsibility in the matter.

"There's only one thing that's holding me back," she said. "I'm afraid that I'll react like Marty did. If I stop accepting the blame for the whole thing, I may become terribly angry at my father. And how do I handle anger at my mother? She's dead!"

I explained to Marsha that she need not be fearful of her anger. It is one of the stages of adjustment that people go through when they are traumatized. In fact, the emotion of anger is the explosive force needed to break out of the prison of denial. When she was ready, we would deal with her anger at her mother.

Marsha didn't argue; she seemed comfortable with the idea that anger could be positive. The important thing now was for her to remember that, though she may have been sexually abused, she no longer had to play out the tempting, though destructive, role of the ruined woman.

---

1. Dr. Mimi Silbert, "Bay Area Prostitutes: Middle Class, 'Good Background,' Sexually Abused," *Current Research on Children,* 2 Vol. (New York: ATCOM, Inc., Publishers, 1983) 2:64.
2. Dr. Alexander T. Simos, "Personal Awareness of 'Filicidal Intent': A Diagnostic Necessity," *Current Research,* 2:44.

Chapter 5

WHEN FORGIVENESS IS NOT ENOUGH

Two months had passed. Marsha faithfully attended the group and participated in it. She even felt comfortable discussing incest and the other forms of abuse the women had experienced.

Through the group she discovered that she was not alone. These women could understand her trauma because they, too, had experienced it. She felt their care, understanding attitudes, and, most of all, their acceptance. She no longer felt isolated and alone, and she was able to discuss her experience without guilt and shame.

When I saw her again privately, she let me know that she told Todd the whole story and all that I had to say about the ruined woman syndrome. His warmth, tenderness and acceptance broke down a big barrier between them. She had been afraid that, if he knew about the incest, he would want nothing to do with her. But his love and acceptance dispelled her fear.

Her relationship with Todd continued to improve. She had become more sexually responsive. And though she occasionally had bouts with the ruined woman syndrome, it was not the problem it once was. But Marsha felt stuck.

"Things are a lot better," she said. "But something keeps hanging on, and I don't know what it is. I've stopped taking the blame for the whole thing, and I realize, at least most of the time, that I'm not a ruined woman. But now I'm angry — furious at my parents for putting me through all of this. It may sound crazy, but I think I'm more angry at my mother than my father."

Marsha was going through a new stage of adjustment. She no longer was denying and avoiding the trauma by accepting the role of the ruined woman. She now was willing to consider the part that her parents played in the trauma. It was a positive step of growth, even though she didn't like feeling angry at them.

"I've been doing a lot of reading about the healing of memories," she told me. "And one thing that they talk about again and again is the need for forgiveness. Maybe the reason I'm so angry is that I haven't forgiven them."

Understanding Forgiveness.

I was encouraged that Marsha was ready to take another step of growth and consider forgiving her parents. But I was concerned that she might think that if she forgave her parents, their relationship would be healed immediately. Because her mother was dead, offering forgiveness to her probably would be the only remedy that would heal that strained and unhappy relationship. But her relationship with her father was another matter. He was still alive.

"Marsha," I said, "if relationships are to be healed, forgiveness is not enough. Those who are forgiven must see their *need* to be forgiven. Many people today continue to be estranged from God because, in spite of God's *offer* of forgiveness, they refuse to accept the fact that they *need* forgiveness. When we put our faith in Christ as the way of salvation, we are also acknowledging our *need* of salvation. Once we are saved, continued fellowship with God is based on confession of our sins. This is made clear in 1 John 1:9, which states 'If we confess our sins, He is faithful and righteous to forgive us our sins and to cleanse us from all unrighteousness.' The word 'confess' in the Greek New Testament means 'to say the same thing.' When we confess our sins, we are saying the same thing about our behavior that God says about it — that it is sin.

"What John is saying here is that God forgave us of all of our sins — past, present, and future — and that this act is vindicated when we confess our sins. We would still be forgiven, even if we didn't confess our sins continually. But there is no *fellowship* with God without confession.

"We see this all the time in parent-child relations. Let's suppose a child lies or steals and is confronted with it by the parent. But the child denies he did anything wrong. The child will not be removed from the family for the offense. Once a child is born into a family, he always will be a member of that family. But his unwillingness to admit his offense against his parents creates a breach of fellowship. They cannot be in fellowship because *they do not agree* about what has been done.

"The original offense is not what grieves the parent. It is the unwillingness of the child to *confess* the wrong. Only through confession — saying the same thing about the offense that the parent is saying — can there be fellowship. It is a proverb of life that two don't walk together unless they are in agreement (Amos 3:3).

"I need to explain this so you won't have any unrealistic expectations about your relationship with your father. I do hope you will reestablish fellowship with him. But you must understand the terms of fellowship. You may be willing to forgive him. But you must be prepared for the possibility that *he may deny* the need to be forgiven anything."

Marsha pondered this in silence. Finally she said, "I was under the impression that if I forgave my parents, I would be released from my anger and that fellowship would be possible."

"That's true," I said. "You can gain release from your anger, and you can experience healing of your wounds. Fellowship *is possible.* But whether or not you enjoy fellowship with your father depends on his willingness to admit his need of forgiveness and to acknowledge that he has wounded you. As far as your mother is concerned, a different approach is needed because she is dead.

"There's a big difference between being released from the pain you have experienced and enjoying fellowship with your dad. Forgiveness releases *you*. Your dad doesn't even have to accept your forgiveness for you to be released from your anger. Indeed, he may even deny that he has anything to be forgiven for. He may become indignant at the very *idea* that there is anything he needs forgiveness for. You should prepare for this possibility."

How Do You Forgive?

Marsha was ready for a major step. She was ready to forgive her parents. She realized that, even if she forgave her dad, he may deny the need for forgiveness.

"How do you go about forgiving your parents for something like this?" she asked.

"First, you need to talk to them about it."

"Talk to them! I can't talk to my mother. She's dead! And I don't know if my dad would talk to me."

"They don't have to be here for you to talk to them. We can imagine that they are here."

"How do you do that?"

"See that empty chair over there? Imagine your dad is sitting there. Create a mental picture — how he's dressed, his posture in the chair, the expression on his face. Once you get a clear picture, I want you to tell him how you feel."

Marsha's body grew tense. "What's the purpose of this?"

"In order to forgive, you need to let go of the pain and anger. And in order to do that, you need to talk directly to your dad about it."

"Do I have to do this? Can't I just tell you how I feel?"

"No. If you did that you'd just be *talking about* your feelings rather than *feeling* your feelings. In order to let go of feelings, we have to get in touch with them. Maybe it would help if I set the stage for you."

I looked at the chair and addressed Marsha's father: "Henry, I've asked you to come here today because Marsha wants to talk to you. She has some feelings that she has never expressed but needs to express if she is to be released from them. What I'd like you to do is just sit there quietly and hear what Marsha has to say."

I then turned to Marsha and said, "Okay, Marsha. Would you tell your dad what you are feeling?"

Marsha looked down at the floor. She sat in silence. Finally, she looked at the chair. But she did not speak.

After a long silence she said, "Dad, I've been wanting to do this for a long time." Silence, and then a deep sigh. "I want to talk about us — uh, about what happened." Long silence, "Dad, did you know what you were doing?"

Marsha looked over at me as though she needed help. As gently as I knew how, I said, "Marsha, you need to say the word. It's okay to say it. The word is 'incest.' "

She looked down at the floor, and slowly her body began to heave with sobs. "It's okay," I said. "Tears have a way of washing away pain."

She let go. In agony she cried, "Oh, God! Help me!" Her body and soul convulsed with all of the torment that she had bottled up for years. It was now as though the dam had burst and there was no controlling the flood of emotions.

There was nothing I could say. I just held her hand and wept with her. I knew that she had to cry until she could cry no more.

Finally, she sat back in her chair and took another tissue to dry her tears. Still looking at the chair, she heaved a great sigh and said the word. "Incest."

She continued looking at the chair as if waiting for her father to answer. Finally, she spoke.

"Did you know that this was what you were doing? I denied it for a long time. And then I tormented myself with blame for the whole thing — for *incest.*"

Her voice broke when she said the word again. But this time the tears didn't come in torrents. She looked away from the chair and stared out the window, as though lost in the memories of her past.

It was some time before she broke the silence. Finally, she turned back to the chair and said, "Dad, I want to *forgive* you."

She could hardly get the last two words out. She sobbed quietly. But, suddenly, it was over. She threw her head back, and in firm even tones said, "I'm not going to torment myself with this any longer. I don't know how alcohol affects people. I don't know if you knew what you were doing. I don't even know if you want forgiveness. But I'm not going to carry this burden any longer. Dad, I'm letting it go. I'm not going to punish myself or you any longer."

"Marsha sat quietly for some time. Then, turning to me, she said with a deep sigh, "I hope that's true. I hope that I don't punish myself or my dad any longer. I know that God has forgiven me. My problem is that I never forgave myself — or my parents."

"Marsha, this has been a good start," I said. "Getting emotional release from something like this is a process. It's like peeling an onion. You take one layer off, and you discover that there's another layer under it — things that you may have forgotten and may need to say to your dad as you did today. And, as happens in peeling onions, you will find that there are yet more tears to shed. But every time you peel a layer off, you are able to get rid of it, at least at the emotional level. You can't change the past. But you can change the way you *feel* about the past."

Marsha had taken a giant step toward further healing. In the weeks to come, she would indeed discover that she had a lot more to say to her father. And each time it would be easier.

Several weeks after her first conversation with her father, she had another significant breakthrough. She returned to the question that she asked her father in the first session: Did he know what he was doing?

I asked her what she thought his answer would be. She surprised me with her matter-of-fact response.

"I think he'd admit that he knew what he was doing. He might cry and beg forgiveness. But you know what? His tears cannot make me feel guilty any more. I *have* forgiven him. Whether or not he has asked God for forgiveness or has forgiven himself, I don't know. I have been out of touch with Dad for years. But this much I know. I have a peace now that I never had before.

"I'm sure that there is more that I haven't dealt with — things that I've forgotten about. And I haven't even begun to deal with my anger at my mother. How do you resolve anger at a person who is dead?"

"Do you know I have the power to raise her from the dead?" I said with a smile.

Marsha smiled, too. "We're going to put her in the chair, huh?"

"Yes."

"Now that will be an experience — talking to the dead!"

"It works. I've done it before."

"I don't doubt it works. I just need a little rest from all of this before I take on Mother. I'm just beginning to get myself back together emotionally, and Todd and I are enjoying our relationship in a way that we've never enjoyed it before. I'm even beginning to enjoy sex! How about that?"

Neither of us was naive enough to believe that all of Marsha's problems were over. But I did agree that she needed a respite from her weekly sessions.

By now it was summertime, and Marsha's group decided that they would not meet during July and August because of vacations. This seemed a good time for a break for all of us. We set a date for September to get together again and review where we were.

Further Steps To Wholeness.

I had not seen Marsha for eight weeks when I got a phone call from California. It was Marsha.

"Surprised to hear from me?"

"Well, yes, as a matter of fact."

"Just wanted to call and give you some good news. Todd and I are here on vacation. I looked up one of my aunts — my dad's sister — and asked her about Dad. She told me he's living here in California and that he's doing well. She said that he has been going to Alcoholics Anonymous and, as far as she knows, he's been dry for some time.

"When she told me he was here in California, I felt I had to see him. Todd agreed that it might help and went along for moral support.

"You wouldn't believe what happened. When we saw each other we both broke into tears and embraced. I didn't have the slightest hesitation about touching him and felt that it truly was a father-daughter embrace and not something incestuous. It was as though he had been sitting in the chair all the time and hearing what I was saying. I found out later that he was working out his own feelings of guilt in AA.

"But the tremendous thing is that we both felt as though we had worked it out together. In talking with the people in his group and with his sponsor privately, he found that he was able to have imaginary conversations with me and tell me how badly he felt for what he had done. And he admitted to me that he knew what he had done. You were right about fellowship and the need to agree.

"I just wanted to tell you — and to let you know that your efforts on me weren't wasted. I think that when I see you in September, I'll be ready to talk to my mother."

The Next Step.

Talking to the dead is no more difficult than talking to the living when they are not present. But how would Marsha know if her mother knew that her father was sexually abusing her? Did she suspect anything? If she did know, why didn't her mother say something?

These were just some of the questions I was sure that Marsha would ask. What kind of answers would we get from beyond the grave?

Chapter 6
THE TAMING OF THE SHREW

September arrived, bringing with it the hope of a respite from the steamy Washington summer. It also brought Marsha hope that she would be able to put to rest the anger she felt toward her mother.

It was the second week of September when she called. "I'm home again," she said cheerfully. "The summer was great, and I'm ready to finish my unfinished business with my mother."

When we met again after her long absence, she filled me in on all of the good things that were happening. She was keeping in touch with her father. She and Todd were doing well, and the visit to her father helped Todd put to rest the anger that he was carrying toward Marsha's father for sexually abusing her.

"Are you ready to tell your mother about your anger?" I asked.

"I don't feel as angry at her as I did several months ago," she said. "But I may be repressing it. You know better than anyone else that I can detach myself emotionally, but I don't want to do this any more. I want to be sure that I've made peace with my mother. Are you ready to help me?"

"Yes, I am. Are you ready?"

"As ready as I'll ever be."

Marsha Talks To Her Mother.

"Let's ask your mother to join us." I paused briefly to create a mental picture of her mother and then said, "Jean, would you have a seat in the chair across from your daughter? Thank you."

Then, looking at the chair, I said, "I've asked you to come here today because Marsha has something she needs to talk to you about. I'd like you to listen quietly to what she says and not interrupt.

"Okay, Marsha. Would you tell your mother what you have on your heart?"

Marsha was remarkably composed, though her body was tense. Quietly, she looked at the chair as she developed a mental picture of her mother.

Finally, she sighed deeply and began. "Mother, I don't know if you knew it or suspected it, but Dad sexually abused me."

Marsha looked at the chair in silence as she gathered her thoughts. "I'm really not sure what I want to say to you. A lot of things are going around in my head right now. I'm curious to know if you knew and, if you did, why you didn't say something about it. Is this why you sent me off to boarding school? Did you really know but take this as a way out?

"Did you know how angry I was with you — and have been for years? Did you know that I couldn't even cry at your funeral? Dad was at your funeral, just drunk as a skunk. I avoided him completely and got out of there as soon as I could.

"We had some home, didn't we? While I was at home going through hell with my father, you were out running all over the country, getting on with your career."

Marsha was beginning to show her anger. She paused again, as if to emphasize what she had said.

"You were always so critical of Dad for being a rotten husband and father. Did you ever stop to take a look at yourself and see what kind of wife and mother *you* were?" Silence.

"I just realized that I don't care whether you knew what was going on or not. The fact of the matter is, whether or not you knew, you did nothing about it — except to send me off to boarding school. I was glad to get away from you and Dad, but do you know how it made me feel? I felt like I was being exiled for doing something wrong. Yes, you gave some grand rationalization about *preparing me* to take care of myself in life. Well, if you wanted to *prepare me* for life, you'd have done a lot better job if you had stayed home!

"It was when I was in boarding school that I first began to feel dirty and ruined. You said that you wanted me to get a good education, but I felt you were punishing me for what I had done with my father, even though there was nothing I could do about it. And I was so mad at you — and still am — because, instead of being there to help me, you punished me by sending me off to school!

"Well, I want you to know that no thanks to you I'm going to be a whole person! I'm going to be a whole person! Do you hear that?"

Marsha looked over at me. "It's strange, but that's about as mad as I can get. I thought I'd rant and rave and cry a lot. But there's nothing there. Just sadness."

The word "sadness" seemed to touch something in her. Tears filled her eyes. She looked back at the chair. Again, there was silence.

Finally, she spoke. "Mom, I do feel sad. I feel sorry for you. Outwardly, you appeared to have it all together. You were upwardly mobile Ms. Executive. But you were a failure as a mother. Dad may have been a failure as a father, but he never pretended to be anything else."

Again, she looked over at me. "I really don't have anything else to say. My anger is gone. I just feel sad."

Through A Glass Darkly.

"How do you think your mother would respond to you if she were sitting in that chair?" I asked.

"I don't know."

Silence.

"Do you think she's with Jesus right now?"

"Yes."

"Do you suppose that they've had any conversations?"

"What do you mean?"

"While you were talking to your mother, I was thinking about the education she must be getting in heaven. A verse in 1 Corinthians 13 keeps coming back to me. I like the language of the King James Version: 'Now we see through a glass darkly' (1 Corinthians 13:12). Paul is saying that truth as we know it now is like a poor reflection in a brass mirror. But when we meet Jesus, we will see the truth clearly and know it fully.

"I don't know if your mother knew when she was alive that your father was abusing you. *But she knows now!* How do you think she responded to the Lord when she found out?"

"She probably defended herself and denied any responsibility for what happened," Marsha replied. "She probably told the Lord, 'I was the very best mother I could be. I didn't know what that drunken pervert of a husband was doing to my daughter!' "

"So what do you suppose the Lord said?"

Marsha's eyes filled with tears. She covered her face with her hand and began to sob. She said in a broken voice, "He told her the *truth!*"

For several minutes her body shook with sobs while she said over and over again, "He told her the *truth!*"

I reached over, took her hand and she looked at me. I said, "Marsha, yes; she does know the truth now."

She squeezed my hand tightly, managed to smile through her tears, and nodded her head, "Yes." Finally, she was able to put it into words: "Yes, she *does* understand now."

"You don't think she's still arguing with the Lord about it?" I asked.

As she dried her tears, Marsha laughed. "Oh, I imagine that she probably gave Him a bad time about it. You'd have to know my mother. I think Shakespeare had her in mind when he wrote *The Taming of the Shrew.* She could back anybody down," Marsha said emphatically. And then softly, "Except the Lord."

Her eyes filled again, and she looked out the window as if to ponder this new image of her mother with the Lord — a shrew who finally had been tamed.

"Not only does your mother know the truth about the past," I said. "Right now she's sitting in heaven's cheering section as one of your biggest fans."

Marsha looked at me quizzically. "What do you mean?"

"In chapter 12 of the Book of Hebrews, the writer paints a picture of a huge stadium filled with spectators cheering on runners who are in a footrace. Marsha, we are those runners running the race of life, and the spectators in the stands are believers who have died and gone to be with Jesus. They're cheering us on.

"Marsha, they're cheering us on because they know how tough the race is. They have run it. But they're cheering with the full confidence that we're going to make it. According to the last verse of 1 Corinthians 13, not only does your mother now know the truth, but she also is filled with faith, hope and love.

"Though your mother didn't seem to care about what happened to you while she was here, she now is filled with hope about your future. Even though she may have done a poor job as a mother, she knows that, by God's power, you will run the race with perseverance.

"I have a fantasy about what your mother might say to you if she were sitting here today. I think she'd say, 'Marsha, I know I wasn't a good mother. I actually abandoned you to your father. I hated being around him, and I felt so stifled, I thought I'd lose my mind sitting at home day after day while he did nothing but drink and pass out on the couch.

" 'But you're right about my rationalizing. I had to give myself, you and my friends a good reason for not being there. I claimed that we needed the money and that I was going to set a good example for my daughter of a parent who makes something of herself. But the truth of the matter is that I hated being trapped in the house with that man so much that I was willing to do anything to get out.' "

When I finished, we sat in silence. Finally Marsha spoke. "Yes, I think she probably would say something like that. You know, it's strange. I always looked at my mother as a strong, 'together' woman. But now I think that all of her bluster, verbiage, intimidation and frantic clawing to the top of the career ladder was her way of dealing with fear. I think that Mother really was a scared little girl dressed up like a grown woman. Scared little girls don't make very good mothers, do they?

"Would it sound arrogant if I said that I think that I'm going to turn out to be a better woman than my mother?"

"Not at all," I replied. "As a father, one of my fondest dreams is that all of my sons will turn out to be better men than I.

"Marsha, this is what hope in the heart of a parent is all about and what your mother is feeling right now. She knows that she made a mess of things. But she also knows that, with God's help, her daughter *will* turn out to be a better woman than she!"

Chapter 7
EPILOGUE

Marsha sent me a Christmas card several months after her last counseling session. She wrote that she was doing very well. In looking back on her recovery she felt that the hardest part had been telling someone what had happened to her.

This correlates with the experience of three other women whom I counseled with the same problem. They all found it very difficult to open up and tell their story, but once they did, they were able to find freedom from their pain and guilt.

I don't mean to suggest that all clients with a history of sexual abuse have been responsive to counseling. What often happens is that a woman will seek counseling offering as the presenting problem guilt, anger, or sexual dysfunction. But when the therapist attempts to get at the root of the problem, she will not reveal a history of sexual abuse.

This has been my experience on a number of occasions. When I strongly suspect a history of sexual abuse, I will raise the subject, tentatively and delicately. I will say, "Perhaps this will shock and anger you, but you sound very much like a woman who was sexually abused as a child." Such an approach is not accusatory, yet it leaves the door open for the woman to disclose her secret as she gains confidence in her therapist.

A colleague recently told me that she is working with a 24-year-old woman who has been in counseling with a variety of therapists since age 14. She has had problems with drugs, rebellion, and self-mutilation — slicing her body with a razor blade.

Just a few days prior to our conversation, the young woman, who had been with her current therapist for two years, finally revealed that she had been sexually abused as a child. She had been in counseling fourteen years, never once disclosing that she had been abused.

A person who has been sexually abused has an incredibly difficult time revealing this to someone else. We must remember that a primary ingredient of sexual abuse is fear — fear of what will happen if the story is known.

A common strategy an abuser uses is to say to the child, 'If you tell your mother what's happening she will say that it's all your fault, she'll divorce me, and I'll go to jail.' Children would rather endure the abuse than run the risk of this happening.

Knowing the likelihood of their parents divorcing over such a disclosure, they carry this fear into adulthood. And they fear they *will be* told it was their fault.

If You Have Been Abused.

If you were sexually abused as a child, it's perfectly understandable that you're having a hard time telling someone. Yet it's imperative that you do. It may be a trusted friend who knows how to listen nonjudgmentally and with caring and understanding. Or, if you're currently in therapy, tell your therapist. If you don't have confidence in your therapist, then find one whom you can tell.

In one study of eight hundred college students who were sexually abused as children, 63 percent of the women and 73 percent of the men had never told anyone about the experience. The silence can have a deadly effect. Though anxiety may be masked for years, the secret is a psychological time-bomb. Guilt, confusion, depression and passivity can suddenly explode into self-destructive behavior, even suicide. Long-term symptoms may include detachment from others, particularly the opposite sex, and frightening flashbacks.[1]

Psychologist Karin C. Meiselman, Ph.D., author of *Incest: A Psychological Study of Causes and Effects with Treatment Recommendations,* says that a victim spends a great deal of energy denying the effects of the abuse. She says, "If you've been betrayed in your most significant early relationships, it's hard to learn how much to trust other people, or to take the risks that are necessary in establishing a lasting relationship."[2]

One of the more frightening aspects of the problem is that women who have been sexually abused as children are a little more likely to sexually abuse their own children. But even more likely is that she will marry a man who sexually abuses *her* daughter.

Why is this? Dr. Meiselman says, "A lot of sexually abused children grow up to become very depressed adults, with low self-esteem. They feel they don't deserve much in relationships, and aren't assertive; if anyone tries to abuse them or their children, they're apt to take it."[3]

To break out of the cycle of "revictimizing," professional help should be sought. The task of the therapist, according to Dr. Meiselman, is to correct the basic misconception that the abuse happened "because I was bad." This, according to Dr. Meiselman, is the key to all the symptoms and problems as the child grows up.[4]

Therapy means dealing with frightening memories and repressed anger. Dr. Meiselman makes an observation that was true in Marsha's case: It's harder to work through anger at a non-abusive mother than an abusive father. "Some patients will say, 'Where was my mother when I needed her? Why didn't she notice the clues I was throwing out?' The victim has to face the uncertainty about whether the mother did know. That's more difficult to work through than anger at the father, who was definitely guilty."[5]

Dr. Meiselman grants that it might be too difficult to express anger at the father directly, but it still can be effectively exorcised. She can express it to her therapist, to supportive friends, or to family members. She says, "The anger often plays itself out. It won't stay with her daily for the rest of her life."[6]

Getting Help.

Suppose someone has a history of sexual abuse? Where do they go for help? How is this problem treated? Parents United is an organization founded to help adults who are abusers. It is a self-help group associated with counseling centers across the country.[7]

It is important, however, to check out any referrals. Individual self-help groups and counseling centers are only as good as the people involved. Check with your pastor to see if he knows anything about the group or the therapist.

The type of therapy offered differs from therapist to therapist. I prefer the method I used with Marsha: Gestalt Therapy. It is action-oriented and gives the client an opportunity to deal with repressed feelings. In many therapies the client is encouraged to talk about the *problem,* which may be a necessary mental exercise. But eventually the therapist must touch the *feelings* of the client and help them deal with unresolved conflict.

But the type of therapeutic approach is not as important as certain qualities found in the therapist. Research into what makes some therapists effective and others ineffective reveals that therapists who are effective possess three qualities called a "therapeutic triad."[8]

The first quality is *genuineness.* An effective therapist is integrated, nondefensive, and authentic in his therapeutic encounters — in a word, genuine.

The second quality is *nonpossessive warmth*. An effective therapist can provide a non-threatening, safe, trusting or secure atmosphere by his acceptance, unconditional positive regard, or love for the client.

The third quality is *accurate empathy.* An effective therapist is able to "be with," "grasp the meaning of," or understand the client on a moment-by-moment basis.[9]

Let's look at each of these in detail for a better understanding of what an abused person should be looking for in a therapist.

1. Genuineness. We tend to distrust people who are artificial and we relate more securely to people who are genuine. We sense this in their ability to relate openly

and not to retreat into facades or roles. This is true in therapy as well as in our daily experience with others.

The therapist who is genuine is not defensive in entering the experience of the client. The therapist is sufficiently well-adjusted so that the client's problems don't uncover unresolved problems in him. As a well-adjusted person he is able to enter the client's experience without becoming angry, impatient, resentful, or make irrational projections and identifications, which are rooted in his own problems. Such negative reactions on the part of the therapist are known as "countertransference."

Sometimes therapists or ministers are people who are afraid to be genuine. The problems the client presents touch that part of their lives that is full of unresolved conflict.

The genuine therapist is intimately acquainted with himself and is able to recognize and accept, as well as respect, both his strengths and weaknesses.[10]

2. Non-possessive Warmth. Warmth is essential to any successful relationship, but it is of crucial importance to a therapeutic relationship where inadequacy, failure, and feelings of guilt riddle the client. Every human being has the need for contact with others. But fear of what others will think often perpetuates their loneliness and isolation.

In the case of an adult who has been suffering from the effects of sexual abuse, the question of acceptance is all-important. The client wonders, "Will this person accept me if I tell him my story?"

The therapist, by his poise, patience, fairness, consistency, rationality, kindliness — in short, his *real* love for the client — is able to create the kind of trust essential to disclosing a secret as painful as sexual abuse. The client must feel free to establish psychological closeness with the therapist, or to put psychological distance between himself and the therapist, without fear of arousing personal affection or offense. The therapist is able to make the client feel secure by remaining friendly, warm, firm and accepting, but avoiding anything that approaches personal entanglement with his client. Even when the client is cool, critical, hostile or provocative, the therapist is able to handle it.

In handling cases of sexual abuse the therapist recognizes that the client feels that they are making a damaging admission when they tell what has happened. He may well reply, "Am I supposed to think badly of you because of that?" The value of this response is that it puts into words the client's anxiety. They most likely feel that the answer to the question is yes.

The next step is for the therapist to ask, "Why should I think badly of you?" At that point they are at the core of the issue.[11]

3. Accurate Empathy. Accurate empathy is the ability to enter the world of the other person's experience and feel it, see it, and hear it as they do. Empathy is in touch with the *feelings* behind what the person is saying rather than the content. The therapist is able to make the client *feel* understood by expressing the client's feelings in his own words. But what he expresses must be *accurate.* He must correctly name the feeling and the degree to which it is being felt.

But the therapist does not come across as though he's examining a specimen. He comes across as an authentic human being who just entered the experience of the client and feels exactly what the client feels.[12]

But where is this kind of therapist found? In addition to Parents United, doctors and ministers often have professional contact with therapists they have confidence in. Have them give you several names, and then call the therapist. He should be willing to give you five minutes of his time to help you "shop" for someone you think can help you.

You will want to know something of his credentials, if he has a specialty, what treatment modalities he uses, and whether or not he can respect your Christian convictions. You will also want to know what his fee is, when it is paid, and whether or not your health insurance covers his services.

When you think you have found a therapist whom you can work with, make an appointment. After your first visit you will be in a better position to know whether or not you will be able to work with him. You will quickly discover whether he has the qualities described above: genuineness, non-possessive warmth, and accurate empathy.

Do not feel that because you went to the therapist once you are obligated to go back. Remember, *you* are the client; *he* is the provider of service. The client always reserves the right to decide whether or not the service is desired. You will find that money spent on one session is well-spent even if you decide not to continue with the therapist.

Other sources of referral are Focus on The Family, P. O. Box 500, Arcadia, CA 91006, (818) 445-1579, The American Association of Marriage and Family Therapists (202) 429-1825, and The American Psychological Association (202) 955-7686. Your pastor is the best referral source, however. He is in touch with professional services in your community and knows who is likely to give you the best service.

If you have been locked up in a prison of guilt and shame it's time that you free yourself. Ask God right now to put you in touch with someone you can talk to. The hardest part is opening the door and trusting someone with your secret.

If after reading this book you want to break the silence by telling me, write or call me. You don't have to tell me who you are. Just by going through the process of breaking your silence you will find it easier to take the next step and get help. My address is 12018 Long Ridge Lane, Bowie, MD 20715, and the phone number is (301) 464-0985. More than anything else I want to give you encouragement and a reason for hope.

---

1. Katie O'Neil, "The Chilling Facts About Sexual Abuse," *Glamour,* (June 1984), p. 265
2. Ibid.
3. Ibid.
4. Ibid.
5. Ibid.
6. Ibid.
7. Parents United, P. O. Box 952, San Jose, CA 95108, (408) 280-5055.

8. Charles B. Truax and Robert R. Carkhuff, *Toward Effective Counseling and Psychotherapy: Training and Practice* (Chicago and New York: Aldine and Atherton, 1972), p. 80.
9. Ibid., p. 3.
10. Ibid., pp. 32-34.
11. Ibid., pp. 34-38.
12. Ibid., pp. 38-42.